Dealing with Feeling....
Jealous

Isabel Thomas

Illustrated by Clare Elsom

Heinemann
LIBRARY

Chicago, Illinois

© 2013 Heinemann Library
an imprint of Capstone Global Library, LLC
Chicago, Illinois

Edited by Dan Nunn, Rebecca Rissman, and
  Catherine Veitch
Designed by Philippa Jenkins
Original illustrations © Clare Elsom
Illustrated by Clare Elsom
Production by Victoria Fitzgerald
Originated by Capstone Global Library, Ltd.
Printed in China

16 15 14 13 12
10 9 8 7 6 5 4 3 2 1

Library of Congress Cataloging-in-Publication Data
Thomas, Isabel, 1980-
 Jealous / Isabel Thomas.
   p. cm.—(Dealing with feeling)
 Includes bibliographical references and index.
 ISBN 978-1-4329-7106-9 (hb)—ISBN 978-1-4329-7115-1 (pb) 1. Jealousy in children—Juvenile literature. 2. Jealousy—Juvenile literature. I. Title.
 BF723.J4T56 2013
 152.4'8—dc23   2012008278

Contents

Some words are shown in bold, **like this**. Find out what they mean in the glossary on page 23.

What Is Jealousy?

shy

worried

angry

happy

Jealousy is a **feeling.** It is normal to have many kinds of feelings every day.

Everyone feels jealous sometimes. You might feel jealous if you think someone else is better than you, or if someone has something you want.

How Do We Know When Someone Is Feeling Jealous?

Our faces and bodies can show other people how we are feeling. **Feelings** can change the way that people behave, too.

Some people may become quiet and sad when they feel jealous. Others may behave badly, even toward their friends and family.

What Does Jealousy Feel Like?

Jealousy can make you feel sad or grumpy that you do not have what other people have.

You might not feel like being nice to people. Trying to hide jealous **feelings** can make you feel worse.

Is It Okay to Feel Jealous?

If your best friend starts playing with new friends, it can make you feel jealous. You might feel sad or angry and say nasty things.

It is okay to feel jealous, but it is not okay to be unkind to somebody. You can learn to deal with jealous **feelings** and be a good friend.

How Can I Deal with Jealousy?

Sometimes jealous **feelings** start because you are worried about something. You might feel worried that your parents do not have enough time to play with you anymore.

The best way to deal with feelings is to talk about them. Share your feelings with your parents or friends. They can help you to feel less jealous.

Why Should I Deal with Jealous Feelings?

Jealousy can make you feel that you are not as good as other people. It can make you behave **unkindly**.

It is okay to feel jealous, but it is
not okay to tease somebody or to
say nasty things about a person.
This will make you feel worse.

What Should I Do When I Feel Jealous of Something?

When someone has something you want, it can make you feel jealous. You might want to take what the person has to make things seem fair.

It is okay to feel jealous, but it is not okay to take or break someone's **property**. Deal with jealous **feelings** by doing something that makes you happy.

What Should I Do When I Feel Jealous of Somebody?

Jealousy can make you feel unhappy when someone else does well. You might feel that you are not good enough.

It is normal to want to do well.
Try to be happy when someone else
does well, too. Be friendly and say,
"Great job!"

How Can I Help Someone Who Is Feeling Jealous?

Remember that everybody feels jealous sometimes. If you notice someone who is feeling jealous, you can help the person feel better.

When you make new friends, remember
to be kind to your old friends, too.
Share what you have with other people,
and they will share things with you.

Make a Jealousy Toolbox

Write down some tips to help you deal with jealous **feelings.**

If someone does something well, say, "Great job!"

Remember that everyone is different. Our differences make us special.

Think about all the things that make you happy.

Remember that you can always feel proud if you have done your best.

Do something you enjoy.

Try not to compare yourself to other people.

Remember that you will get better if you keep trying at something.

Remember all the things you are good at.

Glossary

feeling something that happens inside our minds. It can affect our bodies and the way we behave.

property something that belongs to someone

unkindly in a nasty way. Being unkind to someone can make the person feel sad.

Find Out More

Books

Kravetz, Jonathan. *How to Deal with Jealousy (Let's Work It Out)*. New York: PowerKids, 2007.

Medina, Sarah. *Jealous (Feelings)*. Chicago: Heinemann Library, 2007.

Internet sites

Facthound offers a safe, fun way to find Internet sites related to this book. All of the sites on Facthound have been researched by our staff.

Here's all you do:
Visit www.facthound.com
Type in this code: 9781432971069

Index

24